Farm Alarm

Farm Alarm

poems

Mac Gay

Texas Review Press   ·   Huntsville

Names: Gay, Mac, author.
Title: Farm alarm : poems / by Mac Gay.
Description: Huntsville, Texas : Texas Review Press, [2019] |
Identifiers: LCCN 2019011570 (print) | LCCN 2019014962 (ebook) |
ISBN 9781680031980 (eBook) | ISBN 9781680031881 |
ISBN 9781680031881(pbk.
  :alk. paper)
Subjects: | LCGFT: Poetry.
Classification: LCC PS3607.A9856 (ebook) |
LCC PS3607.A9856 A6 2019 (print) |
  DDC 811/.6—dc23
LC record available at https://lccn.loc.gov/2019011570

Cover Photo: *Some Things Were Kept*, 2013 © Kristina Smith

This book is dedicated to my wife, Jana

CONTENTS

CLOSURE

That's what Dad always wanted.
"Close the door behind you," he'd snap,
or "Did you take out the trash?" The man
hated loose ends, any task dragging
from one day into the next. "You
finish your algebra?" he'd fling at me
blind from behind his newspaper.
Or "Let's finish trimming these hedges
before darkness takes us over."
(Nothing was worse than uneven
Red-tip Photinias.) But the thing
he hated most was getting old:
"Old men are like broken tools
or leaky buckets," he said,
"or the invisible man in the movies,
just fading and fading until he'd
have to wrap himself with rolls of gauze
just so folks would know he was still there."
So Mom took some comfort later
from his bad good luck. That
Sunday morning he left with Bo
to put a neck yoke on the crazy cow
that kept jumping over the fence.
He aimed to be through before church,
and he was, almost: unconscious
as a stone by noon, but
his dawdling heart kept
beating till half past five.

THE LAST WORD

Fifteen and a half and full of it, I was,
and Susan Cooper had asked me to a dance.

Only six months till I get the real thing, Dad.
I have my learner's permit on my hip,
and I can drive as good as you, I said.
Why can't I have the car on Friday night,
instead of you driving us like babies?

Because you are a young ungrateful fool,
I'd tell myself if now could speak to then.

But spoiled and full of piss, I picked a fight
with him on his way to the kitchen
for a glass of milk to calm his ulcer: me.
I wound my anger tight as it would twist
and let it fly full force into that room.
I still can feel our last long hard glare,
and then he turned, all done, back down the hall.
But then, goddamn it, I just couldn't quit;
I hurled *I hate you!* mean as I could yell.
Yet on he walked to bed, then to his
fatal misstep with that crazy cow at dawn.

But fifty years of silence can yell, too.

REAL CHURCHES

Dad or dog, the dead hover.
They make you what you are.
Whether God exists or not,
these are your creators: they
build your walls and dig your wells,
shape your fears, set fires
inside your hells. Cry uncle.
Cry Uncle Clyde, specifically, who
put his hairy hand upon your knee.
He floats before your face today—
a slimy black balloon. Cry Uncle Clyde
was there to shape your darker ways.

Or Dad, who, post his odd demise,
looks at you with his poker face
each time you open morning eyes.
The last words you spoke: *I wish
that you were dead!* And so next
dawn he died, the only blessed time
he did what he was told. He minded
like your best dog in the road,
all eyeballs and entrails you
piled inside the Jim Beam box,
you trailing gore across the road,
leaking from the box's little slot.
Dad or dog, the dead hover—
except in bars, the real churches.

COWBOY DEATH

In those fifties TV shoot-em-ups
it always came to this: catch a bullet,
stiffen, grimace, die. No writhing, no
revolting gore, just instant, painless death.
So when I, callow Southern Baptist boy,
deigned to help our skeletal dying cow
from her pain into cow heaven,
I knew one well-placed twenty-two
between her eyes would work my gift.
But the skulls of large mammals are
(I learned by trial and error) very thick.
After four sharp cracks, she tightened
into one long, drawn-out moan. Then
desperate for the end, I tried another
through her left eye, then the right.
Though blind and bleeding, she,
bless her heart, refused to die.
The entire box of bullets through,
she still survived in a crazy swoon
from my puny hornets' nest.
Fooled by killing's hyperbolic
length and depth, I ran home shaking
in disgust, yet in the quarter hour,
came back stern with larger caliber
to fix my mess's vast diameter
and cleanse away her pain, the both
of us redeemed by higher power.

DAD'S PRIOR COMMITMENT

After Dad was killed, no one came
but the cows when I called.
Old Man Hill let me work on his farm,
but he already had a dear son.
Rattling around the spare world
like a BB in a beer can,
I could stretch in my emptiness
like a liquid filling a crack,
or a rattler that waits in a sack.
I adopted a passive role, waiting
and waiting, like fishing, yet
in all my youth, no bite. Alone
in your head, there's no one to fight
but yourself, till the cows come home.

OUR FATHERLESSNESS

No fence around my foolishness,
I've zigged and zagged from sane
to daft and back again.
I'd steal, bestow, assuage,
then, snap, like lightning, rage.
Dad, back when I was small,
the big Holstein that smashed
your head into that rough barn
wall, she crushed into the nasty
floor my best chance to survive.

Since then I've bounced off all
four walls of night. It's tough
without a dad to point what's right.
Alone, I've fished and fumbled,
flung my head into the jumble,
but the fog has rarely cleared.
I've wasted, wounded, sabotaged
my angel with dumb mumbling.
In Pyrrhic angry back-and-forths
I've laid waste with my tongue.
Seems I just can't win for losing.
Fucking up is not amusing.

In tangled pathless laurel hells,
how many boys lie rotting in the weeds?
The universe seems empty as our
house after you died. Fatherless
means wild, hellacious, lost. Free
tickets to condemned amusement parks.
Rides at these unfair fairs are dangerous.
I fly lone through the dark and dream of us.

CRAP SHOOT

Look back upon the almost-was,
like Pickett's maybe-not-today-
but-thanks-for-asking Charge; or
Truman's going soft on Little Boy;
or Lincoln's nixing theater for cards:
those for-better-or-for-worse
actions aborted, scuttled, revised,
thought the better of,
the life you almost lived,
or lost.

Deep in our woods, we boys
discovered a boggy truck-sized hole
in the wet-weather creek's course
where the clay must have momentarily
forgotten to be impervious,
like a convict's surprising softness
as he courteously opens a door
for some fellow traveler down
the hardscrabble path toward murder.

So after a big rain, we thought
we just might swim some
in that darkish topaz pool
surrounded by the weeds.
Yet it had a snaky look to it,
a snaky feel, holes and roots
receding back into the bank's secrets,
so that even its exotic coolness
and the serendipity of its
being revealed only to us

were not enough to nudge
the near-about forward into history.

But there was the neighbor boy
who later arrived at the same fork
and took the road less traveled
that made all the difference—
for soon he hauled from the hole
his beseeching self, hung with
clinging fits of wrist-thick writhing,
vivid partners in his dance.
He passed before any luck arrived,
his poor choice come up snake eyes.

HOT ROD

James Hancock was not John, but when
James drove he too writ his name large.
Sophomore, a year ahead, he kindly chauffeured
me the twelve miles home some afternoons
after late August football drills. I recall well
his '59 baby blue, moon-hubbed Ford
growling loud and flying east down 36,
James passing cars left and right, no bull,
he did a thing I'd never seen—he passed
cars on the ditch-side of the road. I shit
you not, my friend, and not once hit a sign,
or slid off in the ditch. *Son of a bitch!,*
I mumbled to myself, me, who loved a thrill—
but it wasn't many weeks I heard the tale
which really made me suck my breath, all sick,
of James my wild-ass friend's decapitation
post rear-ending an Old Dominion semi-truck.
The news of James' grave miscalculation
brought shock, but no surprise.
Still, just sixteen, and dead.
And no way round the awful fact
that James' dense, impatient foot
proved swifter than his head.

PRACTICE

"It keeps 'em out of trouble."

Coach Wilbur Fisher

I hated football practice. But it
was a necessary blender: In it
we threw the hormonal demons
of ourselves to be chopped
and spun until all the potentially
lethal juices, the poisons
and the acids, could be mixed
with the healthy air over the green
grass of the fairground in closed
sessions behind chain link.
Bull in the Ring, Oklahoma Drills,
the pitting of one raw soul
against another—best not seen,
like the making of sausage. Yet
those violent discombobulations
were nostalgically worshiped
by our over-the-hill fathers.

Only our mothers could see
the wars raging in our selves,
the blood we drank to survive,
and were frightened by the nerve
of their little supernovas
who could have robbed banks,
slaughtered friends and neighbors,
who could have burned entire
villages, raping the women

and eating the dogs, were it not
for the coaches, with their deep
knowledge of young fire, who
paced daily under the tortuous sun,
hell-bent to tame the damn lions.

RE: THE LOST FARM

That ground once sweetly tenanted...
Robert Penn Warren

Dear Dad,
The farm's changed hands again.
From Shoal Creek Road I saw
they've torn the lot fence down.
Cows graze the seeded row crop land,
yet both of Grandad's barns still stand.
Big colorful machines are everywhere.

Pardon me for selling it. Most
foolish thing I ever did: investing
in the Brooklyn Bridge of poetry
with it. My poems, these crippled things,
don't often fly, yet they're airmail,
of sorts, addressed to you. I hear
their grating whine, and maybe
if that pen of pigs we raised back
then could fly, then so could you.

I write each morning as the others sleep.
Like I was sleeping when you rose
that dawn and left to fix the fence
and yoke the crazy cow that tore it down.
She tore you down forever hence.
Now half a century's silence since,
time's mythologized every single simple
thing. It's made you rise up like a moon
that stares its faint incessant glow.
It makes the farm a promised land,
and when I ask to enter, it says no.

DEMOLITION

When Lennon died and Reagan lived
I took it as bad omen. Young,
pissed, full of righteous fire,
I orbited every grievance with
some version of my No Nukes
sign. The eighties were all
full of poems of mine that
would not fly. I drank too
much. I lost the farm. Our
marriage failed. Demolition,
not construction, was the job
for me. I made a symbol of it,
found it fun to tear
the damn place down.
My favorites were
the chimneys, unused, cold,
with me on fire. I'd start
at the top, armed with a chisel,
hammer, sledge. I'd take
them down the way
my luck was taking me,
in chunks of bricks and dust.
Take that! I'd show, not
tell, with every blow. Each
day I notified the world
of cold and hard: *Goddamn
turnabout's fair play!*

OUR FATHERLESSNESS 2

It's like I've been unplugged, my cord
no longer long enough to reach the wall.

And the house itself, too big: what I thought
warm walls may simply be the sky, still blue,

but now I know the scientific why—
it's just the way our human eyes perceive

cold inhuman wavelengths of the sun's
reflected light, a trick (one of so many),

so that all patriarchal Light devolves
to lowercase, potent as a pile of sticks,

or a sacred rock that's just a plain old rock,
without a brain, a zillion grains of glued,

insensate sand. Which seems all I am headed
for—to add more fertilizer to the soil.

Now with both big and little fathers gone,
no one is here to give a flying fuck.

Without them here, my childish factory
only builds mistakes. Damn sad production.

Old memories twinkle from some now-dead star.
Strange glow from fireflies dead within the jar.

I miss the foolishness I think I always
guessed much less than what the preacher said.

I miss the bread and wine, the whining
prayers that vocalized a kind of yelp.

Though the conversation seemed one-sided,
I loved our loud admission that we needed help.

GHOSTS

Ghosts are holes where folks you knew should be.
Their stoppage stops you exponentially.
For those you hate, death's really not so hard,
but the holes for those you love are large.
Their vacuum takes up acreage in your heart.
Subtraction, not addition, is the part
that disturbs most: ghosts are not things,
they're emptiness; cavities that sting.
All contact's gone, only your love remains.
They leave their haunting memories in our brains.
The silliest holiday is Halloween.
Its jest is revealed often in our teens
when someone dear has died. Gone is all fear—
no spooks. Ghost just means forever never here.

ADVICE

Since you've asked me I must tell you
that this seems not such a good idea;
seems, in fact, much like the botched
euthanasia of the wild puppies
you could not catch or scare away;
ergo, those poorly-placed gut shots
with that vintage British .303 you'd
mail-ordered from Kleins, Chicago
(Lee H. Oswald's favorite store)
that came with armor-piercing ammo,
which, since puppies aren't composed
of steel, simply whisked their bowels
out the other side to hang, as they,
who'd barely just arrived, commenced
their other-worldly arias and tornadic
whirls, and gnawed intestines till
their fires burned mercifully out.
Orchestrating that chaos in the backyard
while Aunt Emily rested after surgery
was to me idiocy heaped on madness.
But I still love you, Brother, adjacent
fruit on our gnarled and withered tree.
And since you've asked, I'll say again,
this also seems no great idea to me.

BLUE YONDER

All left of Uncle Roland is his
God Is My Co-pilot license plate
still testifying on his rusting
wheelless, blocked-up GMC.
I wonder where they flew,
barnstorming wild and low,
dragging whole clotheslines
of the living with them
into the breathless blue.

Nearly three generations
that I've known have flown.
I wonder how one disappears
from fully being here to where
just zero is. Now nothing stands
between me and disappearance
but the clouds, and even buzzards
know they're only air.

When I was eight he shot us
like an arrow through the dizzy breeze
inside his Piper Cub. I giggled
through all his crazy dips and turns.
Back then that wild thin sky was fun.

Now its empty yawning bowl of blue's
turned gray, and all the gods
and uncles that I loved reside inside
of dreams and graves and urns.

AT LAWNWOOD

What a crowd turns up here,
supine beneath this jungle of turf,
shining from these clean stones.
Still, I'm feeling somehow they see
the same blinding blue as me
where heaven once was. All this reputed
repose should comfort, I suppose,
but looking down I'm stopped dead
by dirt. Yet I'll bet when they turn
and sneak a peek down death's abyss
it's like when I survey the top of this pine,
then refocus higher to circling crows,
and again further up to the silver jet.
For surely there's subverted sky in death,
inverted, with deeper niches for profounder
rank; And the hooks of the dead, too,
spectrumed from shallow to deep, wishing
that something, as promised, would bite.
Surely that's what all this silent, still
waiting's about. Some type of fishing.

MURDER HOUSE

I've seen the TV ghost hunters do it:
find the infamous home or madhouse dorm
or ancient prison cell from hell, and sit
and claim tormented human souls ooze out
like spores from toxic mold to nauseate,
chill the air, and terrorize the hunters there.
But here, in spite of all I know about
this house, I'm like an ant in Lincoln's skull—
the walls are there, but all equipment's gone.
And all it sees is hard insensate bone
surrounding air and dust and muted light.
I'm ashamed to say that I almost go
to sleep. The only ghosts I feel are those
of trees split into planks, and freest earth
squeezed into walls of hard, plumb plaster board.
In here I'm pretty sure the deaths have died
and dumbly rest in peace. We're dust to dust;
our torment lies between. In peaceful gilded
autumn light these mindless dust motes mill.
They drift like tiny carefree bloodless sheep
through golden hills of inorganic air.
They gambol down then swirl back up again,
just like they did that sunny murder day.
Dust is dying's meekest circumstance.
Old loss of blood is moot to mindless trance.

SELF-PORTRAIT

Hard rain, but now the sun is out,
and at my feet, a puddle
framing me. But where my brain
should be there is a rock,
dark, allegorical—and all
my dumb life flashes by my eyes
and spawns a knot of queasiness inside.
The black rock tells a sad belated
tale of how, through all this
long-ass life, I've wasted time,
and money, too: like a million pounds
of fresh and golden honey
spilled out on the ground.
Such good green wherewithal,
my father's hard-earned wages,
crumpled like newspaper pages,
and lit to start a panicked fleeting
fire because I felt a fear, a tiny chill.
A thousand goofy jobs. Relationships
run through, chewed up, spit out
like giant packs of Juicy Fruit
buzzed through to suck
the sugar out. This jagged rock
sits heavy where my brain has never been.
Twin brother rock, hard-headed next of kin.

SQUIRREL CREEK FARM

The pecans and the oaks twitched round the place:
Scads of squirrels zoomed through arboreal space.
The acorns and the pecans fed them well,
but fear of fire sent myriad squirrels to hell.
Chewed wires in the attic sealed their fate—
both brothers honed their fear into a hate
that necessitated gunplay in their heads.
They filled up umpteen buckets with the dead
and dumped those once-quick critters in the creek.
(Perhaps the sin's not eating hunted meat.)
That creek was worried red by gunfire's mess,
but what flowed down came back around, I guess:
Just next year, incessant spring rains flooded.
Squirrel Creek swelled, unleashed its repressed id
and swept that hot-wired house clean off its piers.
(I see it float and burn across the years.)
Their mother trapped inside was never found.
Somehow a crazy narrative got round—
some storied, country foolishness, enhanced—
that on its flaming gable, gray squirrels danced.
Both brothers ended in the Asian war.
I guess blood sticks its foot inside death's door.

BLACK HUMOR DOES NOT LIFT,
BUT MAY DISTRACT

My genealogical research
turned and bit me on the ass.
Jasper County records show
we owned sixty slaves.
Who knew? Who'd
want to know? Back
in the day, the day
before the day, actually,
my kin might have sung,
This land is my land,
this land's not your land,
from our big ole mansion
to your run-down shanty.
From the fields we stole
from the Native Americans,
this land was made for me,
not you, had Woody Guthrie
been around for Great-Great-
Great-Granddaddy Sherrod
to snarkily parody. Next he
might have added, *but we do*
have some cotton for you all
to pick, if you'd like to eat again,
or continue to breathe, even.
And with that sterling image
of my forebear, I again
make light of the dark,
laugh to keep from crying,
say something, even if it's nothing
but glib and meaningless noise.
Dark humor does not lift

but may distract. Overturn
and ambiguate the schemas,
so to speak, as does the brisk
shock of any good dead baby
joke. Oh how could the empty
well bucket tied to the end
of my tiny shrinking name have
leaked through so many holes?
Sixty, to be exact. Sixty darkest holes.
It's like Ancestry.com helping
you discover your long lost
German Uncle Adolf. And
the guilt brings no redemption,
just foreknowledge.
Note to myself:
Order flame-resistant t-shirts
for upcoming family reunion
in afterlife.

COBBLER

What would a cobbler say,
ill-suited as he is to this age,
to our baby bartender here?
Struck dumb, I am that cobbler,
or maybe a cooper, or collier—
whatever in hell that is. Heck,
the times have changed, right
under my anachronistic nose.
Buildings are taller, liquor
stronger, girls prettier, but
distant as Mars. The damn
weather itself races only forward,
not marching in place like when
we were boys. Sure, back then
there were arrows on the ends
of time, but time had a mild,
round blankness to it, almost
like a face on which you could
paint a sort of smile, making
the universe gruff but friendly,
because we were made mostly
of future. And when we spied
old men, the silly smiles we
painted on the world looked
back at us from them: They
looked at us, amused, and joked,
and we looked back at them,
amused, nodded our heads
respectfully, and smiled. Then
I thought the eyes of the old men
looked wisely at this world,
easy eyes—nothing like ours now:
scared, and vigilant for death.

MY EARLY MORNING SESSION
WITH THE OWL

Out here near nowhere where we live,
into my open window from
the center of the night came
Who cooks for you?
Right out of Roger Tory Peterson.
Which prompted memories back
some sixty years, deep down Jim Crow.
So in my head I answered that old bird:
"Cora Mae did, and cleaned,
and wiped my little ass when I was small."
Who?
"My other darker mother,
my dearest nursemaid from the past."
My thoughts palavered on:
"She was no slight or trivial influence
on that best part of this spoiled brat's life,"
my dandy smart-ass self half-joked,
parodying Wordsworth, stretching
desperately for comic relief, yet shuddering
at my foolish inability back then
to rightly see the wrongness of those times.
But hindsight's 20/20, as they say,
and the whole sad history of the South
again sifted down upon me in the dark
like a violently shook paperweight's snow.
That lily white only child I was
composed mostly of privileged future
was indeed the star of the show
in our house where Mae served out her time.
More narcissistic than Narcissus,

and like a little Elvis,
I always did it my way,
yes sir, and why not?
A saint cooked for me.
And cleaned. And wiped
my sorry ass when I was small.

ODE TO MEAT

Meat is muscle, right? Like Schwarzenegger's
pec. We carnivores say what the heck,
we're going to eat the part that moves your feet
when you run fast, or maybe savory tissue
that helps you wag your tail. It smells good
on the grill, so good it makes my mind
forget the way you looked with fur, or
back when feathers sailed you through the air.
After we killed you dead, dry lice-filled
feathers just got in the way. Anyway,

flight's over when your purpose shifts
from you to me. You sizzle in a way that makes
me free of how you shone up in the tree
like God's bright thoughts of red or brown or blue;
or ran fast, big and brown, across the ground.
The good Lord lets me catch you with this hound.
The power of your incense from this pan
reiterates meat's good and right and true.
I sit and bow my head and say my grace.
I'm grateful I'm the swine that's eating you.

BULLETIN FROM THE VEGAN GOD

(with attached photo of a man in camo)

When the end comes, and this hunter is dealt
unto the fires, it'll be for the animal murders,
for he's a good Baptist to Baptists, peaceful
as a monk in farmer's clothes. But now
is now, and there's a new Me in charge,
reformed, and when I say do good unto the least,
I mean the least: your kin now run right off
the human scale to beasts. Now vegan
and environmentalist, I see my critters
for what they really are—straight shooters,
pun intended, as loyal to Me as the dust is
to the earth. So with the current glut of grains
and legumes in your bins, sport hunters get
demotions in my new scheme, and birds
and beasts should now be held as more
than just soft delicacies to eat, or blast
away in fun, or mere amorphous blobs
on which to test the Marlin's potency to kill.
This hunter's got a rap sheet longer than
my arm, more bestial than the beasts could
ever be. It started with a .22 and squirrels.
His father paid a nickel for each hide.
And later with his Mauser 98, he turned
wild puppies inside out with blasts
that left their entrails strung across my grass.
The years of calves and pigs he butchered
gave him the gift of heart disease—good

Christian karma finally appeased his slaughterfest.
In his last days he yet hunts dove and quail
and deer. He leaves a trail of clots in fallow fields
where his food plots lure my naïve beasts
for moving target practice. Ever bloody,
he adjusts his warm reward down deeper still.

GUILT

With their quart fruit jars
in September's dusty heat,
the young folks came
to our back spigot for water,
first asking Miss Cora Mae's
permission, then heading back out,
all business, to their cotton sacks
left in the great puzzle-piece
fields of endless brown shot
through with fluffy white stains.

In fourth grade, just off the bus from
school, on our new Zenith in the den
I'd be watching Officer Don
of the ridiculous Popeye Club,
who, seemingly confused
and against all better judgment,
frequently jammed his hand
into the ooey-gooey bag filled
with broken eggs and mud
and chocolate syrup, to the delight
of the giggling peanut gallery—

But oddly I would make a point
to be out of sight when the dark,
unbathed, un-Leave-It-To-Beaver-ish
children from the fields walked
to our house. (How different
our town was from those
Main Streets on TV.)

Something uncomfortable and dark
gnawed at the wiring in the attic
of my head while those children,
excused from their school to pick
our crops, knelt beneath azaleas
in our yard to fill their jars with flat
warm well water from our garden hose.

And yet, distracted by the antics on
our set, I feasted on my milk and Oreos.

FOR BOYS WHO BECOME
THEIR OWN FATHERS

The cracked tailbone taught you to salt
the steps after a storm. Via seven
wrecks you mastered driving trucks.
Thank God or Lady Luck you didn't pack
your parachute yourself. Fucking's fun,
but fucking up is not. And without help
you screwed things up a lot. Still,
goofing up was movement toward the light,
so raise the noose back off your head—
spring practice ain't the game. You,
your puerile enemy, matured to BFF.

Bull-headed orphans learn to be their dads.
Stop picking scabs there in the weeds—
be grateful these mistakes have helped you learn.
You've blundered through youth's hellish
swamp, and bloody here you stand.
What didn't kill you made you strong,
so pin a purple heart upon your ass—
your child called you is almost grown.

Mistakes mark all our growth with scars.
You had to Braille your barbed-wire fences,
stumbling alone there in the dark.
Bear these cuts and amputations proudly.
Trial and error proclaimeth loudly
by your standing here at all.
Celebrate. Present yourself a big bouquet.
Give yourself a hug on Father's Day.

ACKNOWLEDGMENTS

Grateful acknowledgment is made to the editors of the following magazines in which these poems have appeared, some in slightly different form, or with different titles: *Agnes Scott Writer's Festival Magazine*: "Advice"; *Construction*: "Real Churches"; *North of Oxford*: "Closure"; *Snake Nation Review*: "Guilt"; *Texas Poetry Calendar*. "Re. The Lost Farm"; "Closure," "Demolition," and "Practice" appeared in *Pluto's Despair* from Kattywompus Press. "Murder House" received an International Merit Award from *Atlanta Review*.

I would like to thank Loueva Smith, the 2018 Robert Phillips Poetry Prize judge, and the wonderful J. Bruce Fuller and Lisa Tremaine of Texas Review Press. I am also grateful to Beth Gylys and the late Leon Stokesbury for their guidance and support over the years. And most of all, many thanks to my wife Jana for her infinite patience and support.